The Forensic Certified Public Accountant and the Happy New Year Eve's Night in New York

City, New York, United States of America -

Book Number Five

By Dwight David Thrash CPA FCPA CGMA

The characters are fictional, even though they appear to be real. This book is based on real accounting and forensic accounting. The author is a real Certified Public Accountant, Forensic Certified Public Accountant, and a Chartered Global Management Accountant in good standing.

For my parents, Dwight A. and Wanda, & my sister, Delesa and her family,

Thank you, for your support.

I love you.

Contents

New York City, New York, United States of America Mayor Dwight Snowball called me, Titus Uno, Certified Public Accountant, Forensic Certified Public Accountant, and Chartered Global Management Accountant, on my cellphone because the New York City, New York, United States of America Mayor wanted me to assist in the allocation of the New York City, New York, United States of America Funds that are to be used at the New York City, New York, United States New Year Eve and New Year Day events that are sponsored by the New York City, New York, United States of America Government Event Account.

"10, 9, 8, 7, 6, 5, 4, 3, 2, 1, Happy New Year." The Fiscal Year is when a business year ends and a new business year begins. Most Fiscal Years begin and end with the current year end as of December 31st at midnight. So January 1st would be the new fiscal year. However, if the fiscal year is a different month than that month is the business year-end for the company to close their accounts for the new fiscal year.

Miss Leah Two, the New York City Mayor Dwight Snowball's Assistant is over the **Account Number 1231** the New York Eve's Night in New York City, New York, United States of America. I, Titus Uno, Certified Public Accountant, Forensic Certified Public Accountant, and Chartered Global Management Accountant, will be working with Miss Leah Two, the New York City Mayor Dwight Snowball's Assistant to make sure that all of the **Account Number 1231** the New York Eve's Night in New York City, New York, United States of America are properly accounted for and to make sure that the **Account Number 1231** the New York Eve's Night in New York City, New York, United States of America is properly spent so that everyone that is spending the New York Eve's Night in New York City, New York, United States of America is completely satisfied with their New York Eve's Night in New York City, New York, United States of America experience.

Account Number 1231 the New York Eve's Night in New York City, New York, United States of America includes the following Sub-Accounts: **Account Number 1231.01** the New Year Eve's Night at the Empire State Building, **Account Number 1231.02** the New Year Eve's Night at the One World Observatory, **Account Number 1231.03** the New Year Eve's Night at the Statue of Liberty, **Account Number 1231.04** the New Year Eve's Night at Time Square with 2017 New Year Glasses, **Account Number 1231.05** the New Year Eve's Night at Central Park, **Account Number 1231.06** the New Year Eve's Night on a Boat, **Account Number 1231.07** the New Year Eve's Night at the Ice-Skating Rink at the Rockefeller Center, **Account Number 1231.08** the New Year's First Baby Born at Each of the New York City, New York, United States of America Hospitals, **Account Number 1231.09** the New Year Eve's Dances, **Account Number 1231.10** the New Year Eve's Celebrations on Television Every Hour, **Account Number 1231.11** the New Year Eve's Concerts, **Account Number 1231.12** the New Year Eve's Football Games, **Account Number 1231.13** the New Year Eve's Food, **Account Number 1231.14** the New Year's Day Parade, **Account Number 1231.15** the New Year Eve's Fireworks, **Account Number 1231.16** the Midnight Kiss, **Account Number 1231.17** the New Year Eve at an Amusement Park with Extended Hours, **Account Number 1231.18** the New Year Eve's Night at the Movies, **Account Number 1231.19** the New Year Eve's Night at the Museum, **Account Number 1231.20** the New

Year Eve's Night at the Zoo, **Account Number 1231.21** the New Year Eve's Night at Church, **Account Number 1231.22** the New Year Eve's Night in the New York City, New York, United States of America Subway Station, **Account Number 1231.23** the New Year's Resolutions, **Account Number 1231.24** the New Year Eve's Family Night of Games, **Account Number 1231.25** the Clock Strikes Midnight, and **Account Number 1231.26** the Ball Drops at Midnight.

Each of the above Sub-Accounts may be intermingled with each other. The main objective is to make sure that New York City, New York, United States of America Mayor Dwight Snowball is completely satisfied that the **Account Number 1231** the New York Eve's Night in New York City, New York, United States of America and each of the above Sub-Accounts meet their objective and are properly accounted for in the financial statements.

"10, 9, 8, 7, 6, 5, 4, 3, 2, 1, Happy New Year." This year becomes last year as the clock counts down to midnight at the Empire State Building. Kisses are all over the Empire State Building.

Account Number 1231.01 the New Year Eve's Night at the Empire State Building is the first Sub-Account of the **Account Number 1231** the New York Eve's Night in New York City, New York, United States of America.

The Empire State Building is a popular site to view New York City, New York, United States of America when the New Year arrives. The Empire State Building is an iconic symbol of New York City, New York, United States of America and is very visible in the skyline. The fireworks can be seen from the Empire State Building from all four sides since the Empire State Building is such a tall building. Fireworks are so pretty from the view of the Empire State Building in New York City, New York, United States of America.

Everyone likes to go to visit the Empire State Building in New York City, New York, United States of America. There will be food and beverages setup for the people that chooses to be at the Empire State Building in New York City, New York, United States of America to spend New Year Eve and to welcome in the New Year.

I, Titus Uno Certified Public Accountant, Forensic Certified Public Accountant, and Chartered Global Management Accountant, was in New York City, New York, United States of America with my parents and my sister. When my parents, Deuce Uno and Trace Uno, and my sister, Nine Uno, went to the Empire State Building, I was asked by the elevator operator to press the elevator button to carry everyone that was going to the observation level to that floor. I was ten years old when we were in New York City, New York, United States of America for a family vacation. I was so excited to be able to push the elevator button the Empire State Building. It was great to be back in the Empire State Building now that I am older and since I was there with Miss Leah Two, the New York City Mayor Dwight Snowball's Assistant.

I, Titus Uno Certified Public Accountant, Forensic Certified Public Accountant, and Chartered Global Management Accountant, and Miss Leah Two, the New York City Mayor Dwight Snowball's Assistant, decided that we would visit the Empire State Building in New York City, New York, United States of America in order to be able to approve all of the events that are included in the **Account Number 1231.01** the New Year Eve's Night at the Empire State Building, a Sub-Account of the **Account Number 1231** the New York Eve's Night in New York City, New York, United States of America. This is a great time for me, Titus Uno Certified Public Accountant, Forensic Certified Public Accountant, and Chartered Global Management Accountant, and Miss Leah Two, the New York City Mayor Dwight Snowball's Assistant, to perform our job and spend time together at the in New York City, New York, United States of America. I, Titus Uno Certified Public Accountant, Forensic Certified Public Accountant, and Chartered Global Management Accountant, and Miss Leah Two, the New York City Mayor Dwight Snowball's Assistant, enjoy spending time together at the Empire State Building. I, Titus Uno Certified Public Accountant, Forensic Certified Public Accountant, and Chartered Global Management Accountant, and Miss Leah Two, the New York City Mayor Dwight Snowball's

Assistant, have to make sure that all of the events at the Empire State Building in New York City, New York, United States of America are up to the best standards so that everyone that attends this part of the **Account Number 1231** the New York Eve's Night in New York City, New York, United States of America will be very happy that they chose this event to bring in the New Year.

"10, 9, 8, 7, 6, 5, 4, 3, 2, 1, Happy New Year." The One World Observatory is filled with hugs and kisses by those that are in love with each other.

Account Number 1231.02 the New Year Eve's Night at the One World Observatory is the second Sub-Account of the **Account Number 1231** the New York Eve's Night in New York City, New York, United States of America.

The One World Observatory allows the New Year welcomes a special view of New York City, New York, United States of America. This view allows all of the people that are at the One World Observatory to enjoy the food, beverages, decorations, music, and of course, the fireworks that are being presented in New York City, New York, United States of America. This is an awesome site to see all of the fireworks that are being presented in New York City, New York, United States of America.

The One World Observatory means so much to New York City, New York, United States of America. It is so amazing how fast all of the tickets to this event were sold. All of the police departments, fire departments, and emergency departments wanted tickets to show support for The One World Observatory in New York City, New York, United States of America.

The One World Observatory in New York City, New York, United States of America was built to show the world that the United States of America and every other country are not afraid to live life the best way that is possible. In that people should try to make the world a better place to live. That is the reason that "World" is included in the name of this skyscraper "One World Observatory."

I, Titus Uno Certified Public Accountant, Forensic Certified Public Accountant, and Chartered Global Management Accountant, and Miss Leah Two, the New York City Mayor Dwight Snowball's Assistant, decided that we would visit the One World Observatory in New York City, New York, United States of America in order to be able to approve all of the events that are included in the **Account Number 1231.02** the New Year Eve's Night at the One World Observatory, a Sub-Account of the **Account Number 1231** the New York Eve's Night in New York City, New York, United States of America. This is a great time for me, Titus Uno Certified Public Accountant, Forensic Certified Public Accountant, and Chartered Global Management Accountant, and Miss Leah Two, the New York City Mayor Dwight Snowball's Assistant, to perform our job and spend time together at the One World Observatory in New York City, New York, United States of America. I, Titus Uno Certified Public Accountant, Forensic Certified Public Accountant, and Chartered Global Management Accountant, and Miss Leah Two, the New York City Mayor Dwight Snowball's Assistant, enjoy spending time together at the One World Observatory in New York City, New York, United States of America. I, Titus Uno Certified Public Accountant, Forensic Certified Public Accountant, and Chartered Global Management Accountant, and Miss Leah Two, the New York City Mayor Dwight Snowball's Assistant, have to make sure that all of the events at the One World Observatory are up to the best standards so that everyone that attends this part of the **Account Number 1231** the New York Eve's Night in

New York City, New York, United States of America will be very happy that they chose this event to bring in the New Year.

Chapter 4 **Account Number 1231.03** the New Year Eve's Night at the Statue of Liberty

"10, 9, 8, 7, 6, 5, 4, 3, 2, 1, Happy New Year." At midnight, next year becomes this year at the Statue of Liberty. The Statue of Liberty holds her hand up high to bring in the New Year for everyone that calls the United States of America their home.

Account Number 1231.03 the New Year Eve's Night at the Statue of Liberty is the third Sub-Account of the **Account Number 1231** the New Year Eve's Night in New York City, New York, United States of America.

The Statue of Liberty is an excellent site to spend New Year Eve's Night in New York City, New York, United States of America. The Statue of Liberty is such an icon in New York City, New York, United States of America. There are special events that are set up at the Statue of Liberty in New York City, New York, United States of America. The Statue of Liberty in New York City, New York, United States of America offers the people that are spending New Year Eve's night a great view of the fireworks.

I, Titus Uno Certified Public Accountant, Forensic Certified Public Accountant, and Chartered Global Management Accountant, have been to the Statue of Liberty in New York City, New York, United States of America. The Statue of Liberty in New York City, New York, United States of America is such an awesome site to see especially on New Year Eve's night to welcome in the New Year. I enjoyed going to the Statue of Liberty in New York City, New York, United States of

America with my parents, Deuce Uno and Trace Uno, and sister, Nine Uno. My parents, Deuce Uno and Trace Uno, and sister, Nine Uno and myself, Titus Uno Certified Public Accountant, Forensic Certified Public Accountant, and Chartered Global Management Accountant, all had a great time visiting the icon, the Statue of Liberty, in New York City, New York, United States of America.

I, Titus Uno Certified Public Accountant, Forensic Certified Public Accountant, and Chartered Global Management Accountant, and Miss Leah Two, the New York City Mayor Dwight Snowball's Assistant, decided that we would visit the Empire State Building in order to be able to approve all of the events that are included in the **Account Number 1231.03** the New Year Eve's Night at the Statue of Liberty, a Sub-Account of the **Account Number 1231** the New York Eve's Night in New York City, New York, United States of America. This is a great time for me, Titus Uno Certified Public Accountant, Forensic Certified Public Accountant, and Chartered Global Management Accountant, and Miss Leah Two, the New York City Mayor Dwight Snowball's Assistant, to perform our job and spend time together at the Statue of Liberty in New York City, New York, United States of America. I, Titus Uno Certified Public Accountant, Forensic Certified Public Accountant, and Chartered Global Management Accountant, and Miss Leah Two, the New York City Mayor Dwight Snowball's Assistant, enjoy spending time together at the Statue of Liberty. I, Titus Uno Certified Public Accountant, Forensic Certified Public Accountant, and Chartered Global Management Accountant, and Miss Leah Two, the New York City Mayor Dwight Snowball's Assistant, have to make sure that all of the events at the Statue of Liberty in New York City, New York, United States of America are up to the best standards so that everyone that attends this part of the **Account Number 1231** the New York Eve's Night in

New York City, New York, United States of America will be very happy that they chose this

event to bring in the New Year.

"10, 9, 8, 7, 6, 5, 4, 3, 2, 1, Happy New Year." The Time Square is filled with New Year visitors to welcome the New Year in New York City, New York, United States of America.

I, Titus Uno Certified Public Accountant, Forensic Certified Public Accountant, and Chartered Global Management Accountant, and Miss Leah Two, the New York City Mayor Dwight Snowball's Assistant, decided that we would visit Time Square, together. The New York City Mayor Dwight Snowball is going to attend the Time Square Ball Dropping. In fact, the New York City Mayor Dwight Snowball is going to push the button that drops the Time Square Ball at Midnight.

Account Number 1231.04 the New Year Eve's Night at Time Square with 2017 New Year Glasses is the fourth Sub-Account of the **Account Number 1231** the New York Eve's Night in New York City, New York, United States of America.

Time Square is a very special place to be on New Year Eve's night because that is where the ball drops. There is a chance that the people that are at Time Square might actually get to appear on the television as the crowd waits for the ball to drop every hour in the United States of America. It is party, party, and party every hour in the United States of America as the ball is dropped four times for each of the four time-zones that are in the United States of America. It is excited to celebrate for each of the four time-zones, no matter where you are in the United States of America.

I, Titus Uno Certified Public Accountant, Forensic Certified Public Accountant, and Chartered Global Management Accountant, and Miss Leah Two, the New York City Mayor Dwight Snowball's Assistant, decided that we would visit the Empire State Building in order to be able to approve all of the events that are included in the **Account Number 1231.04** the New Year Eve's Night at Time Square with 2017 New Year Glasses, a Sub-Account of the **Account Number 1231** the New York Eve's Night in New York City, New York, United States of America. This is a great time for me, Titus Uno Certified Public Accountant, Forensic Certified Public Accountant, and Chartered Global Management Accountant, and Miss Leah Two, the New York City Mayor Dwight Snowball's Assistant, to perform our job and spend time together at the Time Square in New York City, New York, United States of America. I, Titus Uno Certified Public Accountant, Forensic Certified Public Accountant, and Chartered Global Management Accountant, and Miss Leah Two, the New York City Mayor Dwight Snowball's Assistant, enjoy spending time together at the Time Square in New York City, New York, United States of America. I, Titus Uno Certified Public Accountant, Forensic Certified Public Accountant, and Chartered Global Management Accountant, and Miss Leah Two, the New York City Mayor Dwight Snowball's Assistant, have to make sure that all of the events at the Time Square in New York City, New York, United States of America are up to the best standards so that everyone that attends this part of the **Account Number 1231** the New York Eve's Night in New York City, New York, United States of America will be very happy that they chose this event to bring in the New Year with their 2017 New Year Glasses.

I, Titus Uno Certified Public Accountant, Forensic Certified Public Accountant, and Chartered Global Management Accountant, and Miss Leah Two, the New York City Mayor Dwight Snowball's Assistant, really enjoyed wearing our 2017 New Year Glasses to test them out before the real dropping of the Ball occurs.

Chapter 6 Account Number 1231.05 the New Year Eve's Night at Central Park

"10, 9, 8, 7, 6, 5, 4, 3, 2, 1, Happy New Year." Central Park is a great site to be as the New Year starts and the fireworks are being fired into the New York City, New York, United States of America sky.

Account Number 1231.05 the New Year Eve's Night at Central Park is the fifth Sub-Account of the **Account Number 1231** the New York Eve's Night in New York City, New York, United States of America.

Central Park is loaded with events to bring in the New Year. There are sports events, music events, romantic events, family events, and relaxing events that people can participate in to bring in the New Year.

Sports events include walking, jogging, running, skateboarding, bike riding, basketball, tennis, walking the dog, throwing a football or baseball, rowing boats, and playing Frisbee Golf.

Music events includes individual people playing music to professional concerts. People also may have their ear pods. Music is so exciting to listen to as the New Year arrives in New York City, New York, United States of America.

Romantic events involve doing an activity with your date to bring in the New Year. It is so reciting to have a date on New Year. You are assured of getting a romantic kiss when the New Year arrives.

Family events allows the entire family to bring in the New Year doing fun activities with the entire family. It is great to bring in the New Year with the entire family in Central Park while participating in the events that are available.

Relaxing events allows people to relax and take a nap to relaxing and watching the stars if the sky is fair. Some people relax on a blanket or in a chair. Others just stand and look around at what is happening in Central Park.

I, Titus Uno Certified Public Accountant, Forensic Certified Public Accountant, and Chartered Global Management Accountant, and Miss Leah Two, the New York City Mayor Dwight Snowball's Assistant, decided that we would visit Central Park in order to be able to approve all of the events that are included in the **Account Number 1231.05** the New Year Eve's Night at Central Park, a Sub-Account of the **Account Number 1231** the New York Eve's Night in New York City, New York, United States of America. This is a great time for me, Titus Uno Certified Public Accountant, Forensic Certified Public Accountant, and Chartered Global Management Accountant, and Miss Leah Two, the New York City Mayor Dwight Snowball's Assistant, to perform our job and spend time together in Central Park. I, Titus Uno Certified Public Accountant, Forensic Certified Public Accountant, and Chartered Global Management Accountant, and Miss Leah Two, the New York City Mayor Dwight Snowball's Assistant, enjoy spending time together in Central Park. I, Titus Uno Certified Public Accountant, Forensic Certified Public Accountant, and Chartered Global Management Accountant, and Miss Leah Two, the New York City Mayor Dwight Snowball's Assistant, have to make sure that all of the events in Central Park are up to the best standards so that everyone that attends this part of the **Account Number 1231** the New York Eve's Night in New York City, New York, United States

of America will be very happy that they chose this event to bring in the New Year.

"10, 9, 8, 7, 6, 5, 4, 3, 2, 1, Happy New Year."

Account Number 1231.06 the New Year Eve's Night on a Boat Airplane, Helicopter, or even a Blimp is the sixth Sub-Account of the **Account Number 1231** the New York Eve's Night in New York City, New York, United States of America.

Boats are a great way to spend the evening and night when the New Year arrives in New York City, New York, United States of America. This gives a great view of New York City, New York, United States of America from the water when the New Year arrives. The water allows the people to enjoy the water by using a boat to party and to observe all of the New York City, New York, United States of America fireworks.

Airplanes are a great way to spend the evening and night when the New Year arrives in New York City, New York, United States of America. This gives a great view of New York City, New York, United States of America from the air when the New Year arrives. The air allows the people to enjoy the view of New York City, New York, United States of America by using an airplane to party and to observe all of the New York City, New York, United States of America fireworks.

Helicopters are a great way to spend the evening and night when the New Year arrives in New York City, New York, United States of America. This gives a great view of New York City,

New York, United States of America from the air when the New Year arrives. The air allows the people to enjoy the view of New York City, New York, United States of America by using a Helicopter to party and to observe all of the New York City, New York, United States of America fireworks.

Blimps are a great way to spend the evening and night when the New Year arrives in New York City, New York, United States of America. This gives a great view of New York City, New York, United States of America from the air when the New Year arrives. The air allows the people to enjoy the view of New York City, New York, United States of America by using a blimp to party and to observe all of the New York City, New York, United States of America fireworks. The air allows the people to enjoy the view of New York City, New York, United States of America by using an airplane to party and to observe all of the New York City, New York, United States of America fireworks.

I, Titus Uno Certified Public Accountant, Forensic Certified Public Accountant, and Chartered Global Management Accountant, and Miss Leah Two, the New York City Mayor Dwight Snowball's Assistant, decided that we would visit all of the New York City, New York, United States of America in a Boat, Airplane, Helicopter, and even a Blimp in order to be able to approve all of the events that are included in the **Account Number 1231.06** the New Year Eve's Night on a Boat Airplane, Helicopter, or even a Blimp, a Sub-Account of the **Account Number 1231** the New York Eve's Night in New York City, New York, United States of America. This is a great time for me, Titus Uno Certified Public Accountant, Forensic Certified Public Accountant, and Chartered Global Management Accountant, and Miss Leah Two, the New York City Mayor Dwight Snowball's Assistant, to perform our job and spend time together in a Boat Airplane,

Helicopter, or even a Blimp. I, Titus Uno Certified Public Accountant, Forensic Certified Public Accountant, and Chartered Global Management Accountant, and Miss Leah Two, the New York City Mayor Dwight Snowball's Assistant, enjoy spending time together in a Boat Airplane, Helicopter, or even a Blimp. I, Titus Uno Certified Public Accountant, Forensic Certified Public Accountant, and Chartered Global Management Accountant, and Miss Leah Two, the New York City Mayor Dwight Snowball's Assistant, have to make sure that all of the events in a Boat Airplane, Helicopter, or even a Blimp are up to the best standards so that everyone that attends this part of the **Account Number 1231** the New York Eve's Night in New York City, New York, United States of America will be very happy that they chose this event to bring in the New Year.

"10, 9, 8, 7, 6, 5, 4, 3, 2, 1, Happy New Year." The Ice-Skating Rink at the Rockefeller Center is a fun and exciting place to be when the New Year arrives

Account Number 1231.07 the New Year Eve's Night at the Ice-Skating Rink at the Rockefeller Center is the seventh Sub-Account of the **Account Number 1231** the New York Eve's Night in New York City, New York, United States of America.

The Ice-Skating Rink at the Rockefeller Center is a great site to welcome in the New Year in New York City, New York, United States of America. The Ice-Skating Rink at the Rockefeller Center is a very popular and famous icon in New York City, New York, United States of America. This is a place that families can carry their families and have fun skating to welcome in the New Year.

The Ice-Skating Rink at the Rockefeller Center is the site of a famous golden statue that is above the Ice-Skating Rink at the Rockefeller Center. This statue is very pretty and is very recognizable to everyone that sees the statue.

The Ice-Skating Rink at the Rockefeller Center is also the site of the big Christmas tree that is setup above the Ice-Skating Rink at the Rockefeller Center and above the golden statue. This tree is so big that it takes a crane to place the Christmas tree in the proper place. It takes several days from unloading the Christmas tree until the Christmas tree is completely decorated so the all of the people that attend the Ice-Skating Rink at the Rockefeller Center can enjoy this magnificent Christmas tree.

I, Titus Uno Certified Public Accountant, Forensic Certified Public Accountant, and Chartered Global Management Accountant, and Miss Leah Two, the New York City Mayor Dwight Snowball's Assistant, decided that we would visit the Ice-Skating Rink at the Rockefeller Center in order to be able to approve all of the events that are included in the **Account Number 1231.07** the New Year Eve's Night at the Ice-Skating Rink at the Rockefeller Center, a Sub-Account of the **Account Number 1231** the New York Eve's Night in New York City, New York, United States of America. This is a great time for me, Titus Uno Certified Public Accountant, Forensic Certified Public Accountant, and Chartered Global Management Accountant, and Miss Leah Two, the New York City Mayor Dwight Snowball's Assistant, to perform our job and spend time together at Ice-Skating Rink at the Rockefeller Center. I, Titus Uno Certified Public Accountant, Forensic Certified Public Accountant, and Chartered Global Management Accountant, and Miss Leah Two, the New York City Mayor Dwight Snowball's Assistant, enjoy spending time together at the Ice-Skating Rink at the Rockefeller Center. I, Titus Uno Certified Public Accountant, Forensic Certified Public Accountant, and Chartered Global Management Accountant, and Miss Leah Two, the New York City Mayor Dwight Snowball's Assistant, have to make sure that all of the events at Ice-Skating Rink at the Rockefeller Center are up to the best standards so that everyone that attends this part of the **Account Number 1231** the New York Eve's Night in New York City, New York, United States of America will be very happy that they chose this event to bring in the New Year.

"10, 9, 8, 7, 6, 5, 4, 3, 2, 1, Happy New Year." The music plays and plays while the dancers dance. It is fun to have a dance on New Year's. The time passes very fast while dancing or listening to the music.

Account Number 1231.08 the New Year's First Baby Born at Each of the New York City, New York, United States of America Hospitals is the eighth Sub-Account of the **Account Number 1231** the New York Eve's Night in New York City, New York, United States of America.

The New Year's First Baby Born at Each of the New York City, New York, United States of America Hospitals is usually given a very special prepared package of gifts filled with items that the New Year's First Baby Born at Each of the New York City, New York, United States of America Hospitals can use. There is usually a picture take at each of the New York City, New York, United States of America Hospitals. Each of the New York City, New York, United States of America Hospitals really enjoys celebrating the New Year's First Baby Born at Each of the New York City, New York, United States of America Hospitals. This is a really exciting time for the New Year's First Baby Born at each of the New York City, New York, United States of America Hospitals

I, Titus Uno Certified Public Accountant, Forensic Certified Public Accountant, and Chartered Global Management Accountant, and Miss Leah Two, the New York City Mayor Dwight Snowball's Assistant, decided that we would visit each of the New York City, New York, United States of America Hospital in order to be able to approve all of the events that are included in the **Account Number 1231.08** the New Year's First Baby Born at Each of the New York City, New York, United States of America Hospitals, a Sub-Account of the **Account Number 1231** the New York Eve's Night in New York City, New York, United States of America. This is a great time for me, Titus Uno Certified Public Accountant, Forensic Certified Public Accountant, and Chartered Global Management Accountant, and Miss Leah Two, the New York City Mayor Dwight Snowball's Assistant, to perform our job and spend time together at each of the New York City, New York, United States of America Hospital. I, Titus Uno Certified Public Accountant, Forensic Certified Public Accountant, and Chartered Global Management Accountant, and Miss Leah Two, the New York City Mayor Dwight Snowball's Assistant, enjoy spending time together at each of the New York City, New York, United States of America Hospital. I, Titus Uno Certified Public Accountant, Forensic Certified Public Accountant, and Chartered Global Management Accountant, and Miss Leah Two, the New York City Mayor Dwight Snowball's Assistant, have to make sure that all of the events at each of the New York City, New York, United States of America Hospital are up to the best standards so that everyone that attends this part of the **Account Number 1231** the New York Eve's Night in New York City, New York, United States of America will be very happy that they chose this event to bring in the New Year.

"10, 9, 8, 7, 6, 5, 4, 3, 2, 1, Happy New Year." The music plays and plays while the dancers dance. It is fun to have a dance on New Year's. The time passes very fast while dancing or listening to the music.

Account Number 1231.09 the New Year Eve's Dances is the ninth Sub-Account of the **Account Number 1231** the New York Eve's Night in New York City, New York, United States of America.

The New Year Eve's Dances are very famous in New York City, New York, United States of America. The most famous dance is the Disco Dance that is held New Year Eve in New York City, New York, United States of America that is a dance-off. The dancers dance as long as they can until a judge taps their shoulder to signal that their participation in this dance-off is completed. The last pair of dancers that are left dancing wins. This is one example of in New York City, New York, United States of America New Year Eve's dance. There are several New Year Eve Dances in New York City, New York, United States of America.

I, Titus Uno Certified Public Accountant, Forensic Certified Public Accountant, and Chartered Global Management Accountant, and Miss Leah Two, the New York City Mayor Dwight Snowball's Assistant, decided that we would visit the New Year Eve's Dances in order to be able to approve all of the events that are included in the **Account Number 1231.09** the New Year Eve's Dances, a Sub-Account of the **Account Number 1231** the New York Eve's Night in New York City, New York, United States of America. This is a great time for me, Titus Uno Certified

Public Accountant, Forensic Certified Public Accountant, and Chartered Global Management Accountant, and Miss Leah Two, the New York City Mayor Dwight Snowball's Assistant, to perform our job and spend time together at the New Year Eve's Dances. I, Titus Uno Certified Public Accountant, Forensic Certified Public Accountant, and Chartered Global Management Accountant, and Miss Leah Two, the New York City Mayor Dwight Snowball's Assistant, enjoy spending time together at the New Year Eve's Dances. I, Titus Uno Certified Public Accountant, Forensic Certified Public Accountant, and Chartered Global Management Accountant, and Miss Leah Two, the New York City Mayor Dwight Snowball's Assistant, have to make sure that all of the events at the New Year Eve's Dances are up to the best standards so that everyone that attends this part of the **Account Number 1231** the New York Eve's Night in New York City, New York, United States of America will be very happy that they chose this event to bring in the New Year.

"10, 9, 8, 7, 6, 5, 4, 3, 2, 1, Happy New Year." The television is a great ways to welcome in the New Year.

Account Number 1231.10 the New Year Eve's Celebrations on Television Every Hour is the tenth Sub-Account of the **Account Number 1231** the New York Eve's Night in New York City, New York, United States of America.

The New Year Eve's Celebrations on Television Every Hour is a very awesome way to welcome in the New Year. This is so exciting to people all over the United States of America. The ball dropping that is in Time Square in New York City, New York, United States of America is a very popular site that people all over the world tune in to watch every New Year Eve's Night. No matter what people are doing they tune in at each of the hour ball dropping that is in Time Square in New York City, New York, United States of America.

New Year Eve's Celebrations on Television Every Hour that is in Time Square in New York City, New York, United States of America is planned down to the precise second. This event is so exciting to watch on the television. It is always the number one watched event by everyone that is welcoming in the New Year by watching the television.

Over the years it was just on the television, but now people can even watch this event on their cellphone, their laptop, or even on their computer thanks to the internet. These figures also have to be added into the above figures. Technology is great.

People can attend events in New York City, New York, United States of America and still be able to watch the New Year Eve's Celebrations on Television Every Hour on one of their gadgets. These gadgets have changed the entire way people can welcome in the New Year. These people can attend one event and watch other events at the same time.

I, Titus Uno Certified Public Accountant, Forensic Certified Public Accountant, and Chartered Global Management Accountant, and Miss Leah Two, the New York City Mayor Dwight Snowball's Assistant, decided that we would visit the New Year Eve's Celebrations in order to be able to approve all of the events that are included in the **Account Number 1231.10** the New Year Eve's Celebrations, a Sub-Account of the **Account Number 1231** the New York Eve's Night in New York City, New York, United States of America. This is a great time for me, Titus Uno Certified Public Accountant, Forensic Certified Public Accountant, and Chartered Global Management Accountant, and Miss Leah Two, the New York City Mayor Dwight Snowball's Assistant, to perform our job and spend time together at the New Year Eve's Celebrations. I, Titus Uno Certified Public Accountant, Forensic Certified Public Accountant, and Chartered Global Management Accountant, and Miss Leah Two, the New York City Mayor Dwight Snowball's Assistant, enjoy spending time together at the New Year Eve's Celebrations. I, Titus Uno Certified Public Accountant, Forensic Certified Public Accountant, and Chartered Global Management Accountant, and Miss Leah Two, the New York City Mayor Dwight Snowball's Assistant, have to make sure that all of the events at the New Year Eve's Celebrations are up to the best standards so that everyone that attends this part of the **Account Number 1231** the New York Eve's Night in New York City, New York, United States of America will be very happy that they chose this event to bring in the New Year.

"10, 9, 8, 7, 6, 5, 4, 3, 2, 1, Happy New Year." There are several concerts that are put into place to help people welcome in the New Year with their loved ones. Music is a great way to start the New Year, especially in New York City, New York, United States of America.

Account Number 1231.11 the New Year Eve's Concerts is the eleventh Sub-Account of the **Account Number 1231** the New York Eve's Night in New York City, New York, United States of America.

The New Year Eve's Concerts are a very musical way to welcome in the New Year in New York City, New York, United States of America. The people attend the concert of their choosing and then watch the New York City, New York, United States of America fireworks. These concert can be performed both indoors or outside. Either way the concerts are always very entertaining to the people attending the concerts.

The New Year Eve's Concerts are an excellent way for couples to spend New Year Eve's night in New York City, New York, United States of America. It is always exciting to hear music. To hear music on New Year Eve's night in New York City, New York, United States of America is very romantic and awesome.

There are also several musicals that can be attended New Year Eve's night in New York City, New York, United States of America. These musicals have actors that can also sing their parts. Some of these musicals are very popular and are sold out every night. This New Year Eve's night is made extra special for those that attend these musicals on New Year Eve's night in New

York City, New York, United States of America. These musicals have been sold out for months so those that attend have had this event planned for months. These events are so exciting to attend and then the New York City, New York, United States of America fireworks are ready to be presented for everyone to watch.

The New York City, New York, United States of America fireworks are setup so that everyone that is in New York City, New York, United States of America can observe the New York City, New York, United States of America fireworks.

I, Titus Uno Certified Public Accountant, Forensic Certified Public Accountant, and Chartered Global Management Accountant, and Miss Leah Two, the New York City Mayor Dwight Snowball's Assistant, decided that we would visit the New Year Eve's Concerts in order to be able to approve all of the events that are included in the **Account Number 1231.11** the New Year Eve's Concerts, a Sub-Account of the **Account Number 1231** the New York Eve's Night in New York City, New York, United States of America. This is a great time for me, Titus Uno Certified Public Accountant, Forensic Certified Public Accountant, and Chartered Global Management Accountant, and Miss Leah Two, the New York City Mayor Dwight Snowball's Assistant, to perform our job and spend time together at the New Year Eve's Concerts. I, Titus Uno Certified Public Accountant, Forensic Certified Public Accountant, and Chartered Global Management Accountant, and Miss Leah Two, the New York City Mayor Dwight Snowball's Assistant, enjoy spending time together at the New Year Eve's Concerts. I, Titus Uno Certified Public Accountant, Forensic Certified Public Accountant, and Chartered Global Management Accountant, and Miss Leah Two, the New York City Mayor Dwight Snowball's Assistant, have to make sure that all of the events at the New Year Eve's Concerts are up to the best standards so that everyone that attends this part of the **Account Number 1231** the New York Eve's Night in New York City, New York, United States of America will be very happy that they chose this event to bring in the New Year.

Chapter 13 **Account Number 1231.12** the New Year Eve's Football Games

"10, 9, 8, 7, 6, 5, 4, 3, 2, 1, Happy New Year." These football games can be watched at the football stadium or may be watched on the television.

Account Number 1231.12 the New Year Eve's Football Games is the twelfth Sub-Account of the **Account Number 1231** the New York Eve's Night in New York City, New York, United States of America.

I, Titus Uno Certified Public Accountant, Forensic Certified Public Accountant, and Chartered Global Management Accountant, and Miss Leah Two, the New York City Mayor Dwight Snowball's Assistant, decided that we would visit the station that are showing the New Year Eve's Football Games on the television to help with advertising for the other Sub-Accounts in order to be able to approve all of the events that are included in the **Account Number 1231.12** the New Year Eve's Football Games, a Sub-Account of the **Account Number 1231** the New York Eve's Night in New York City, New York, United States of America. This is a great time for me, Titus Uno Certified Public Accountant, Forensic Certified Public Accountant, and Chartered Global Management Accountant, and Miss Leah Two, the New York City Mayor Dwight Snowball's Assistant, to perform our job and spend time together at the station that are showing the New Year Eve's Football Games on the television to help with advertising for the other Sub-Accounts: **Account Number 1231.01** the New Year Eve's Night at the Empire State Building, **Account Number 1231.02** the New Year Eve's Night at the One World Observatory,

Account Number 1231.03 the New Year Eve's Night at the Statue of Liberty, **Account Number 1231.04** the New Year Eve's Night at Time Square with 2017 New Year Glasses, **Account Number 1231.05** the New Year Eve's Night at Central Park, **Account Number 1231.06** the New Year Eve's Night on a Boat, **Account Number 1231.07** the New Year Eve's Night at the Ice-Skating Rink at the Rockefeller Center, **Account Number 1231.08** the New Year's First Baby Born at Each of the New York City, New York, United States of America Hospitals, **Account Number 1231.09** the New Year Eve's Dances, **Account Number 1231.10** the New Year Eve's Celebrations on Television Every Hour, **Account Number 1231.11** the New Year Eve's Concerts, **Account Number 1231.13** the New Year Eve's Food, **Account Number 1231.14** the New Year's Day Parade, **Account Number 1231.15** the New Year Eve's Fireworks, **Account Number 1231.16** the Midnight Kiss, **Account Number 1231.17** the New Year Eve at an Amusement Park with Extended Hours, **Account Number 1231.18** the New Year Eve's Night at the Movies, **Account Number 1231.19** the New Year Eve's Night at the Museum, **Account Number 1231.20** the New Year Eve's Night at the Zoo, **Account Number 1231.21** the New Year Eve's Night at Church, **Account Number 1231.22** the New Year Eve's Night in the New York City, New York, United States of America Subway Station, **Account Number 1231.23** the New Year's Resolutions, **Account Number 1231.24** the New Year Eve's Family Night of Games, **Account Number 1231.25** the Clock Strikes Midnight, and **Account Number 1231.26** the Ball Drops at Midnight. are up to the best standards so that everyone that attends this part of the **Account Number 1231** the New York Eve's Night in New York City, New York, United States of America will be very happy that they chose this event to bring in the New Year.

"10, 9, 8, 7, 6, 5, 4, 3, 2, 1, Happy New Year." There are so many foods that people think is great to have at New Year time.

Cabbage and black eyed peas are thought to bring the eater great luck and lots of money. Coins are placed in the pot while cooking, but taken out before eating the cabbage and black eyed peas. If it not taken out before eating, the on that finds the coin might have to visit the dentist. It is common sense to take the coins out before eating.

Cooked ham goes great with the cabbage and black eyed peas. Chocolate pies are a great ending to the New Year's meal. Some people even make relish trays and meat with cheese trays as appetizers before the big New Year's meal.

Account Number 1231.13 the New Year Eve's Food is the thirteenth Sub-Account of the **Account Number 1231** the New York Eve's Night in New York City, New York, United States of America.

The New Year Eve's Food is very important to every event. These events would be very going without the New Year Eve's night food. These foods offer the people attending the events a chance to share this food with others that they are attending these events with while eating great food.

Some people have their favorite New Year Eve's night food ranging from chips and dips to black eyed peas and cabbage to lobsters to fish and chips. Some of these foods are thought to bring the eater luck in the New Year. "10, 9, 8, 7, 6, 5, 4, 3, 2, 1, Happy New Year to the ones that you love."

Food is a great way to welcome in the New Year. It is great to break bread with the ones that you love. Spending time with the ones that you love is a very special way to welcome in this New Year. Kissing the ones that you love tells them that you are very happy to start the New Year with those that you love.

I, Titus Uno Certified Public Accountant, Forensic Certified Public Accountant, and Chartered Global Management Accountant, and Miss Leah Two, the New York City Mayor Dwight Snowball's Assistant, decided that we would visit the restaurants New Year Eve's Food in order to be able to approve all of the events that are included in the **Account Number 1231.13** the New Year Eve's Food, a Sub-Account of the **Account Number 1231** the New York Eve's Night in New York City, New York, United States of America. This is a great time for me, Titus Uno Certified Public Accountant, Forensic Certified Public Accountant, and Chartered Global Management Accountant, and Miss Leah Two, the New York City Mayor Dwight Snowball's Assistant, to perform our job and spend time together at restaurants New Year Eve's Food. I, Titus Uno Certified Public Accountant, Forensic Certified Public Accountant, and Chartered Global Management Accountant, and Miss Leah Two, the New York City Mayor Dwight Snowball's Assistant, enjoy spending time together at the restaurants New Year Eve's Food. I, Titus Uno Certified Public Accountant, Forensic Certified Public Accountant, and Chartered Global Management Accountant, and Miss Leah Two, the New York City Mayor Dwight Snowball's Assistant, have to make sure that all of the events at the restaurants New Year Eve's Food are up to the best standards so that everyone that attends this part of the **Account**

Number 1231 the New York Eve's Night in New York City, New York, United States of America

will be very happy that they chose this event to bring in the New Year.

"10, 9, 8, 7, 6, 5, 4, 3, 2, 1, Happy New Year." The Rose Bowl parade is exciting to watch while cooking the big New Year's meal. It is so exciting to watch this parade that has floats that are made from flowers and seeds. People spend weeks working on these floats. You can see all the love that goes into these floats.

There are several big bands that march in this parade. Including the two bands that are from the 2 Universities that are playing in the Rose Bowl that year. These bowl game parades are exciting to watch.

New York City, New York, United States of America always has a parade that goes down 34th Street. This is a very elaborate parade that consists of horses, bands, floats, celebrities, and of course it ends with Santa Claus and his famous reindeer. Santa Claus waves at the people at the parade. The people all throw ticker tape to mark the end of the parade as Santa Claus passes by. The ticker tape is also dropped from the skyscrapers.

Horses are a part of the New York City, New York, United States of America New Year's parade. There are several parade participants that include horses. From military and police to rodeo and private horse riders. All of the horses are so pretty.

Bands are a part of the New York City, New York, United States of America New Year's parade. These bands come from all over the United States of America and from all over the world. The bands show how talented musician they are. Most bands have held fundraisers to be able to attend the New York City, New York, United States of America New Year's parade.

Floats are a part of the New York City, New York, United States of America New Year's parade. These floats have taken days to be ready for the parade. The floats have to be able to support all the people that are on these floats.

Celebrities are a part of the New York City, New York, United States of America New Year's parade. These celebrities add to the awesomeness of the New York City, New York, United States of America New Year's parade.

Santa Claus and his famous reindeer are a part of the New York City, New York, United States of America New Year's parade. Santa Claus is the perfect ending to the New York City, New York, United States of America New Year's parade.

Account Number 1231.14 the New Year's Day Parade is the fourteenth Sub-Account of the **Account Number 1231** the New York Eve's Night in New York City, New York, United States of America.

I, Titus Uno Certified Public Accountant, Forensic Certified Public Accountant, and Chartered Global Management Accountant, and Miss Leah Two, the New York City Mayor Dwight Snowball's Assistant, decided that we would visit the route of the New Year Parade in New York City, New York, United States of America in order to be able to approve all of the events that are included in the **Account Number 1231.14** the New Year's Day Parade, a Sub-Account of the **Account Number 1231** the New York Eve's Night in New York City, New York, United States of America. This is a great time for me, Titus Uno Certified Public Accountant, Forensic Certified Public Accountant, and Chartered Global Management Accountant, and Miss Leah Two, the New York City Mayor Dwight Snowball's Assistant, to perform our job and spend time together at the site of the New Year's Day Parade. I, Titus Uno Certified Public Accountant, Forensic Certified Public Accountant, and Chartered Global Management Accountant, and Miss Leah Two, the New York City Mayor Dwight Snowball's Assistant, enjoy spending time together at the site of the New Year's Day Parade. I, Titus Uno Certified Public Accountant, Forensic Certified Public Accountant, and Chartered Global Management Accountant, and Miss Leah Two, the New York City Mayor Dwight Snowball's Assistant, have to make sure that all of the events at the site of the New Year's Day Parade are up to the best standards so that everyone that attends this part of the **Account Number 1231** the New York Eve's Night in New York City, New York, United States of America will be very happy that they chose this event to bring in the New Year.

"10, 9, 8, 7, 6, 5, 4, 3, 2, 1, Happy New Year." The fireworks show is part of the New Year tradition. Fireworks are fired all over New York City, New York, United States of America. People love to watch fireworks as the New Year arrives.

Account Number 1231.15 the New Year Eve's Fireworks is the fifteenth Sub-Account of the **Account Number 1231** the New York Eve's Night in New York City, New York, United States of America.

The New Year Eve's Fireworks are a very important part of the New York City, New York, United States of America celebration. All of the **Account Number 1231** the New York Eve's Night in New York City, New York, United States of America includes the following Sub-Accounts: **Account Number 1231.01** the New Year Eve's Night at the Empire State Building, **Account Number 1231.02** the New Year Eve's Night at the One World Observatory, **Account Number 1231.03** the New Year Eve's Night at the Statue of Liberty, **Account Number 1231.04** the New Year Eve's Night at Time Square with 2017 New Year Glasses, **Account Number 1231.05** the New Year Eve's Night at Central Park, **Account Number 1231.06** the New Year Eve's Night on a Boat, **Account Number 1231.07** the New Year Eve's Night at the Ice-Skating Rink at the Rockefeller Center, **Account Number 1231.08** the New Year's First Baby Born at Each of the New York City, New York, United States of America Hospitals, **Account Number 1231.09** the New Year Eve's Dances, **Account Number 1231.10** the New Year Eve's Celebrations on Television Every Hour, **Account Number 1231.11** the New Year Eve's Concerts, **Account**

Number 1231.12 the New Year Eve's Football Games, **Account Number 1231.13** the New Year Eve's Food, **Account Number 1231.14** the New Year's Day Parade, **Account Number 1231.16** the Midnight Kiss, **Account Number 1231.17** the New Year Eve at an Amusement Park with Extended Hours, **Account Number 1231.18** the New Year Eve's Night at the Movies, **Account Number 1231.19** the New Year Eve's Night at the Museum, **Account Number 1231.20** the New Year Eve's Night at the Zoo, **Account Number 1231.21** the New Year Eve's Night at Church, **Account Number 1231.22** the New Year Eve's Night in the New York City, New York, United States of America Subway Station, **Account Number 1231.23** the New Year's Resolutions, **Account Number 1231.24** the New Year Eve's Family Night of Games, **Account Number 1231.25** the Clock Strikes Midnight, and **Account Number 1231.26** the Ball Drops at Midnight, offer events that are improved by the New Year Eve's Fireworks.

I, Titus Uno Certified Public Accountant, Forensic Certified Public Accountant, and Chartered Global Management Accountant, and Miss Leah Two, the New York City Mayor Dwight Snowball's Assistant, decided that we would visit the best sites to view the Fireworks in order to be able to approve all of the events that are included in the **Account Number 1231.15** the New Year Eve's Fireworks a Sub-Account of the **Account Number 1231** the New York Eve's Night in New York City, New York, United States of America. This is a great time for me, Titus Uno Certified Public Accountant, Forensic Certified Public Accountant, and Chartered Global Management Accountant, and Miss Leah Two, the New York City Mayor Dwight Snowball's Assistant, to perform our job and spend time together at the sites of the New Year Eve's Fireworks. I, Titus Uno Certified Public Accountant, Forensic Certified Public Accountant, and Chartered Global Management Accountant, and Miss Leah Two, the New York City Mayor

Dwight Snowball's Assistant, enjoy spending time together at the sites of the New Year Eve's Fireworks. I, Titus Uno Certified Public Accountant, Forensic Certified Public Accountant, and Chartered Global Management Accountant, and Miss Leah Two, the New York City Mayor Dwight Snowball's Assistant, have to make sure that all of the events at the sites of the New Year Eve's Fireworks are up to the best standards so that everyone that attends this part of the **Account Number 1231** the New York Eve's Night in New York City, New York, United States of America will be very happy that they chose this event to bring in the New Year.

"10, 9, 8, 7, 6, 5, 4, 3, 2, 1, Happy New Year." Then the couples that are together kiss. This marks a great beginning to the New Year.

Account Number 1231.16 the Midnight Kiss is the sixteenth Sub-Account of the **Account Number 1231** the New York Eve's Night in New York City, New York, United States of America.

All of the **Account Number 1231** the New York Eve's Night in New York City, New York, United States of America includes the following Sub-Accounts: **Account Number 1231.01** the New Year Eve's Night at the Empire State Building, **Account Number 1231.02** the New Year Eve's Night at the One World Observatory, **Account Number 1231.03** the New Year Eve's Night at the Statue of Liberty, **Account Number 1231.04** the New Year Eve's Night at Time Square with 2017 New Year Glasses, **Account Number 1231.05** the New Year Eve's Night at Central Park, **Account Number 1231.06** the New Year Eve's Night on a Boat, **Account Number 1231.07** the New Year Eve's Night at the Ice-Skating Rink at the Rockefeller Center, **Account Number 1231.08** the New Year's First Baby Born at Each of the New York City, New York, United States of America Hospitals, **Account Number 1231.09** the New Year Eve's Dances, **Account Number 1231.10** the New Year Eve's Celebrations on Television Every Hour, **Account Number 1231.11** the New Year Eve's Concerts, **Account Number 1231.12** the New Year Eve's Football Games, **Account Number 1231.13** the New Year Eve's Food, **Account Number 1231.14** the New Year's Day Parade, **Account Number 1231.15** the New Year Eve's Fireworks, **Account Number 1231.17** the New Year Eve at an Amusement Park with Extended Hours, **Account Number 1231.18** the

New Year Eve's Night at the Movies, **Account Number 1231.19** the New Year Eve's Night at the Museum, **Account Number 1231.20** the New Year Eve's Night at the Zoo, **Account Number 1231.21** the New Year Eve's Night at Church, **Account Number 1231.22** the New Year Eve's Night in the New York City, New York, United States of America Subway Station, **Account Number 1231.23** the New Year's Resolutions, **Account Number 1231.24** the New Year Eve's Family Night of Games, **Account Number 1231.25** the Clock Strikes Midnight, and **Account Number 1231.26** the Ball Drops at Midnight, are improved by hanging the New Year's Mistletoe that will lead to the Midnight Kiss. However, the New Year's Mistletoe was not necessary now in order to be kissed by the ones that you love.

I, Titus Uno Certified Public Accountant, Forensic Certified Public Accountant, and Chartered Global Management Accountant, and Miss Leah Two, the New York City Mayor Dwight Snowball's Assistant, decided that we would visit the Romantic Places that the Midnight Kisses might occur in order to be able to approve all of the events that are included in the **Account Number 1231.16** the Midnight Kiss a Sub-Account of the **Account Number 1231** the New York Eve's Night in New York City, New York, United States of America. This is a great time for me, Titus Uno Certified Public Accountant, Forensic Certified Public Accountant, and Chartered Global Management Accountant, and Miss Leah Two, the New York City Mayor Dwight Snowball's Assistant, to perform our job and spend time together at the sites of the Midnight Kiss. I, Titus Uno Certified Public Accountant, Forensic Certified Public Accountant, and Chartered Global Management Accountant, and Miss Leah Two, the New York City Mayor Dwight Snowball's Assistant, enjoy spending time together at the sites of the Midnight Kiss. I, Titus Uno Certified Public Accountant, Forensic Certified Public Accountant, and Chartered

Global Management Accountant, and Miss Leah Two, the New York City Mayor Dwight Snowball's Assistant, have to make sure that all of the events at the sites of the Midnight Kiss are up to the best standards so that everyone that attends this part of the **Account Number 1231** the New York Eve's Night in New York City, New York, United States of America will be very happy that they chose this event to bring in the New Year.

"10, 9, 8, 7, 6, 5, 4, 3, 2, 1, Happy New Year." The amusement parks are still open at New Year to bring in the New Year on a great note. These amusement parks are open late to give the crowds that attend these amusement parks a chance to start the New Year off with fun things to do.

Account Number 1231.17 the New Year Eve at an Amusement Park with Extended Hours is the seventeenth Sub-Account of the **Account Number 1231** the New York Eve's Night in New York City, New York, United States of America.

The New Year Eve's night at an Amusement Park with Extended Hours for the Amusement Parks that are in New York City, New York, United States of America. The Amusement Park rides are so exciting to ride before watching the New York City, New York, United States of America fireworks. These rides include a rollercoaster, a Ferris wheel, a joust-about or a scrambler, a train, a tall slide, and other fun and exciting rides.

The New Year Eve's night at an Amusement Park with Extended Hours for the Amusement Parks that are in New York City, New York, United States of America, also includes carnival games. These carnival games include games such as make a basket with a basketball, knock down all of the cans that are setup, or shoot the targets with a gun. If you win you get a prize. How exciting is that. You win a prize to start the New Year?

I, Titus Uno Certified Public Accountant, Forensic Certified Public Accountant, and Chartered Global Management Accountant, have been to many amusement parks over the years. These amusement parks are so exciting.

To ride the rides and to play the carnival games, before watching the New York City, New York, United States of America fireworks. What a way to start a New Year.

I, Titus Uno Certified Public Accountant, Forensic Certified Public Accountant, and Chartered Global Management Accountant, and Miss Leah Two, the New York City Mayor Dwight Snowball's Assistant, decided that we would visit the Amusement Parks in order to be able to approve all of the events that are included in the **Account Number 1231.17** the New Year Eve at an Amusement Park with Extended Hours a Sub-Account of the **Account Number 1231** the New York Eve's Night in New York City, New York, United States of America. This is a great time for me, Titus Uno Certified Public Accountant, Forensic Certified Public Accountant, and Chartered Global Management Accountant, and Miss Leah Two, the New York City Mayor Dwight Snowball's Assistant, to perform our job and spend time together at the New Year Eve at an Amusement Park with Extended Hours. I, Titus Uno Certified Public Accountant, Forensic Certified Public Accountant, and Chartered Global Management Accountant, and Miss Leah Two, the New York City Mayor Dwight Snowball's Assistant, enjoy spending time together at the New Year Eve at an Amusement Park with Extended Hours. I, Titus Uno Certified Public Accountant, Forensic Certified Public Accountant, and Chartered Global Management Accountant, and Miss Leah Two, the New York City Mayor Dwight Snowball's Assistant, have to make sure that all of the events at the New Year Eve at an Amusement Park with Extended Hours are up to the best standards so that everyone that attends this part of the **Account**

Number 1231 the New York Eve's Night in New York City, New York, United States of America

will be very happy that they chose this event to bring in the New Year.

"10, 9, 8, 7, 6, 5, 4, 3, 2, 1, Happy New Year." The museum is an awesome place to bring in the New Year. The museum stays open all night so that adults and children can spend the night observing the exhibits with their family and friends.

Account Number 1231.18 the New Year Eve's Night at the Movies is the eighteenth Sub-Account of the **Account Number 1231** the New York Eve's Night in New York City, New York, United States of America.

The New Year Eve's Night at the Movies in New York City, New York, United States of America is another option for people to choose to do on New Year Eve's night. There are always movies to choose to watch before the fireworks are presented.

Movies are always exciting to watch, but add the fact that it might start in one year and end the next year. These movies are an option to watch on New Year Eve's night. Why not pick a movie to watch on New Year Eve's night with you family.

I, Titus Uno Certified Public Accountant, Forensic Certified Public Accountant, and Chartered Global Management Accountant, stayed at a hotel one year that showed a movie on a wall in a restaurant so that the children could watch the movie to start the New Year. This was a very smart and exciting idea for the children. The children had something that they could do to bring in the New Year. These children had the best time watching the movie with their parents to start the New Year together.

These movies also include the concession stand. Some theaters include popcorn and drinks in a preset value package for New Year Eve's night. These packages help make the New Year Eve's night at the Movies an enjoyable for the movie watchers. Movies help make New Year Eve's night pass very fast for the people that are spending their New Year Eve's night at the movies.

I, Titus Uno Certified Public Accountant, Forensic Certified Public Accountant, and Chartered Global Management Accountant, and Miss Leah Two, the New York City Mayor Dwight Snowball's Assistant, decided that we would visit the Movie Theaters in order to be able to approve all of the events that are included in the **Account Number 1231.18** the New Year Eve's Night at the Movie, a Sub-Account of the **Account Number 1231** the New York Eve's Night in New York City, New York, United States of America. This is a great time for me, Titus Uno Certified Public Accountant, Forensic Certified Public Accountant, and Chartered Global Management Accountant, and Miss Leah Two, the New York City Mayor Dwight Snowball's Assistant, to perform our job and spend time together at the Movies. I, Titus Uno Certified Public Accountant, Forensic Certified Public Accountant, and Chartered Global Management Accountant, and Miss Leah Two, the New York City Mayor Dwight Snowball's Assistant, enjoy spending time together at the Movies. I, Titus Uno Certified Public Accountant, Forensic Certified Public Accountant, and Chartered Global Management Accountant, and Miss Leah Two, the New York City Mayor Dwight Snowball's Assistant, have to make sure that all of the events at the Movies are up to the best standards so that everyone that attends this part of the

Account Number 1231 the New York Eve's Night in New York City, New York, United States of America will be very happy that they chose this event to bring in the New Year.

"10, 9, 8, 7, 6, 5, 4, 3, 2, 1, Happy New Year." The museum is an awesome place to bring in the New Year.

Account Number 1231.19 the New Year Eve's Night at the Museum is the nineteenth Sub-Account of the **Account Number 1231** the New York Eve's Night in New York City, New York, United States of America.

Museums are great places to welcome the New Year. Museums are filled with exhibits that people can learn from about the exhibits. Hours upon hours can be spent in a museum. Most museums will show movies that people can watch.

Museums also have tours that people can take in order to assist in the learning about the exhibits. These exhibits are so interesting. There is so much that can be learned from these exhibits.

I, Titus Uno Certified Public Accountant, Forensic Certified Public Accountant, and Chartered Global Management Accountant, have spent hours inside if museums. These museums are filled with history and information.

Museums include artwork, statues, furniture, pottery, artifacts, dinosaurs, and animals such as turtles. Turtles are interesting animals. Some are tiny while some are large. Some of the artwork is priceless. Some of the furniture has been used by famous people. Most of the exhibits are items that were used by people long ago in the past. This past is exciting to study and learn from in order to make our future a better one. This is also called learning from the past to make a great future. Past events and items do allow for the people that study and learn from these items to alter their future.

I, Titus Uno Certified Public Accountant, Forensic Certified Public Accountant, and Chartered Global Management Accountant, and Miss Leah Two, the New York City Mayor Dwight Snowball's Assistant, decided that we would visit the Museums in order to be able to approve all of the events that are included in the **Account Number 1231.19** the New Year Eve's Night at the Museum, a Sub-Account of the **Account Number 1231** the New York Eve's Night in New York City, New York, United States of America. This is a great time for me, Titus Uno Certified Public Accountant, Forensic Certified Public Accountant, and Chartered Global Management Accountant, and Miss Leah Two, the New York City Mayor Dwight Snowball's Assistant, to perform our job and spend time together at the Museum. I, Titus Uno Certified Public Accountant, Forensic Certified Public Accountant, and Chartered Global Management Accountant, and Miss Leah Two, the New York City Mayor Dwight Snowball's Assistant, enjoy spending time together at the Museum. I, Titus Uno Certified Public Accountant, Forensic Certified Public Accountant, and Chartered Global Management Accountant, and Miss Leah Two, the New York City Mayor Dwight Snowball's Assistant, have to make sure that all of the events at the Museum are up to the best standards so that everyone that attends this part of the **Account Number 1231** the New York Eve's Night in New York City, New York, United States of America will be very happy that they chose this event to bring in the New Year.

"10, 9, 8, 7, 6, 5, 4, 3, 2, 1, Happy New Year." The animals are so excited to bring in the New Year along with the human visitors. All of the animals get to stay up late and even get a special treat.

Account Number 1231.20 the New Year Eve's Night at the Zoo is the twentieth Sub-Account of the **Account Number 1231** the New York Eve's Night in New York City, New York, United States of America.

Zoos are very interesting sites to welcome the New Year. Zoos offer both children and adults adventure while learning about the animals at the zoo. The animals really enjoy it when people are around.

Zoos offer interesting adventures called "Zoo-Thousand and Seventeen". These adventures carry the people that are at the zoo on a great learning tour. All of the animals are decked out in their "Zoo-Thousand and Seventeen" costumes along with the "Zoo-Thousand and Seventeen" guides. These "Zoo-Thousand and Seventeen" guides explain interesting facts about all of the "Zoo-Thousand and Seventeen" animals. Everyone involved in the "Zoo-Thousand and Seventeen" adventures has the vest time, including the "Zoo-Thousand and Seventeen" animals. Happy "Zoo-Thousand and Seventeen" is a great program that can be continued every year in the "Zoo-Thousands." Of course, next year will be "Zoo-Thousand and Eighteen."

The zoos even offer "Zoo-Thousand and Seventeen" fireworks that the people at the zoo can watch to bring in the New Year. These fireworks are really pretty. The fireworks incorporate smiling animals in the presentations. These fireworks improve in their design every year.

This year is going to even include a laser show that also includes animals in the presentation. These laser shows are going to continue every year and will keep growing and improving. "Zoo-Thousand and Seventeen" is a great program for the zoo. You will see animal such as lions, tigers, giraffes, snakes, turtles (like the one on the cover of this book), spiders, birds, hippopotamus, rhinoceros, bears, or even monkeys.

I, Titus Uno Certified Public Accountant, Forensic Certified Public Accountant, and Chartered Global Management Accountant, and Miss Leah Two, the New York City Mayor Dwight Snowball's Assistant, decided that we would visit the Zoo in order to be able to approve all of the events that are included in the **Account Number 1231.20** the New Year Eve's Night at the Zoo a Sub-Account of the **Account Number 1231** the New York Eve's Night in New York City, New York, United States of America. This is a great time for me, Titus Uno Certified Public Accountant, Forensic Certified Public Accountant, and Chartered Global Management Accountant, and Miss Leah Two, the New York City Mayor Dwight Snowball's Assistant, to perform our job and spend time together at the Zoo. I, Titus Uno Certified Public Accountant, Forensic Certified Public Accountant, and Chartered Global Management Accountant, and Miss Leah Two, the New York City Mayor Dwight Snowball's Assistant, enjoy spending time together at the Zoo. I, Titus Uno Certified Public Accountant, Forensic Certified Public Accountant, and Chartered Global Management Accountant, and Miss Leah Two, the New York City Mayor Dwight Snowball's Assistant, have to make sure that all of the events at the Zoo are up to the best standards so that everyone that attends this part of the **Account Number 1231** the New York Eve's Night in New York City, New York, United States of America will be very happy that they chose this event to bring in the New Year.

Happy "Zoo-Thousand and Seventeen."

"10, 9, 8, 7, 6, 5, 4, 3, 2, 1, Happy New Year." The church is the only place some people go to bring in the New Year.

Account Number 1231.21 the New Year Eve's Night at Church is the twenty-first Sub-Account of the **Account Number 1231** the New York Eve's Night in New York City, New York, United States of America.

The New Year Eve's Night at Church is a site that religious people love to attend to welcome in the New Year. Some churches offer New Year Eve's night at their church.

Churches are a great place to be when the New Year begins. There are different events going on at the churches such as singing, praying, talking, playing, watching the television, and planning the events for the New Year. There is food and beverages also available. This is also a great place for single adults to have activities to do together in a great environment. I, Titus Uno, Certified Public Accountant, Forensic Certified Public Accountant, and Chartered Global Management Accountant, am away from my Single Adults Ministries Class, but I know that my Class will have fun while I am in New York City, New York, United States of America.

Some people love to start the New Year at church.

I, Titus Uno Certified Public Accountant, Forensic Certified Public Accountant, and Chartered Global Management Accountant, and Miss Leah Two, the New York City Mayor Dwight

Snowball's Assistant, decided that we would visit the Churches in order to be able to approve all of the events that are included in the **Account Number 1231.21** the New Year Eve's Night at Church, a Sub-Account of the **Account Number 1231** the New York Eve's Night in New York City, New York, United States of America. This is a great time for me, Titus Uno Certified Public Accountant, Forensic Certified Public Accountant, and Chartered Global Management Accountant, and Miss Leah Two, the New York City Mayor Dwight Snowball's Assistant, to perform our job and spend time together at different Churches in New York City, New York, United States of America. I, Titus Uno Certified Public Accountant, Forensic Certified Public Accountant, and Chartered Global Management Accountant, and Miss Leah Two, the New York City Mayor Dwight Snowball's Assistant, enjoy spending time together at different Churches in New York City, New York, United States of America. I, Titus Uno Certified Public Accountant, Forensic Certified Public Accountant, and Chartered Global Management Accountant, and Miss Leah Two, the New York City Mayor Dwight Snowball's Assistant, have to make sure that all of the events at different Churches in New York City, New York, United States of America are up to the best standards so that everyone that attends this part of the **Account Number 1231** the New York Eve's Night in New York City, New York, United States of America will be very happy that they chose this event to bring in the New Year.

"10, 9, 8, 7, 6, 5, 4, 3, 2, 1, Happy New Year."

Account Number 1231.22 the New Year Eve's Night in the New York City, New York, United States of America Subway Station is the twenty-second Sub-Account of the **Account Number 1231** the New York Eve's Night in New York City, New York, United States of America.

At every stop along the New York City, New York, United States of America Subway Station there has strategically been placed musician including singers, bands, and soloists. These singers and musicians all has been approved and have the proper permits. The New York City, New York, United States of America Subway Station riders can hear the music and singers as they stop at every stop along their ride in the New York City, New York, United States of America Subway Station. These singers and musicians have an opportunity to gain a great fan base from playing at an event like this. Everyone involved seems to be very excited.

Some bands might even be able to say that this event was the event that made their band famous. This is so cool to help give great bands a slot in this event to give the band or choir great exposure in a big audience.

I, Titus Uno Certified Public Accountant, Forensic Certified Public Accountant, and Chartered Global Management Accountant, and Miss Leah Two, the New York City Mayor Dwight Snowball's Assistant, decided that we would visit the Subway Station in order to be able to approve all of the events that are included in the **Account Number 1231.22** the New Year Eve's Night in the New York City, New York, United States of America Subway Station, a Sub-Account of the **Account Number 1231** the New York Eve's Night in New York City, New York, United States of America. This is a great time for me, Titus Uno Certified Public Accountant, Forensic Certified Public Accountant, and Chartered Global Management Accountant, and Miss Leah Two, the New York City Mayor Dwight Snowball's Assistant, to perform our job and spend time together at the New York City, New York, United States of America Subway Station. I, Titus Uno Certified Public Accountant, Forensic Certified Public Accountant, and Chartered Global Management Accountant, and Miss Leah Two, the New York City Mayor Dwight Snowball's Assistant, enjoy spending time together at the New York City, New York, United States of America Subway Station. I, Titus Uno Certified Public Accountant, Forensic Certified Public Accountant, and Chartered Global Management Accountant, and Miss Leah Two, the New York City Mayor Dwight Snowball's Assistant, have to make sure that all of the events at the New York City, New York, United States of America Subway Station are up to the best standards so that everyone that attends this part of the **Account Number 1231** the New York Eve's Night in New York City, New York, United States of America will be very happy that they chose this event to bring in the New Year.

"10, 9, 8, 7, 6, 5, 4, 3, 2, 1, Happy New Year." Most people make New Year's Resolutions. Some are hard to keep while others are easy to keep.

Account Number 1231.23 the New Year's Resolutions is the twenty-third Sub-Account of the **Account Number 1231** the New York Eve's Night in New York City, New York, United States of America.

The following Sub-Accounts: **Account Number 1231.01** the New Year Eve's Night at the Empire State Building, **Account Number 1231.02** the New Year Eve's Night at the One World Observatory, **Account Number 1231.03** the New Year Eve's Night at the Statue of Liberty, **Account Number 1231.04** the New Year Eve's Night at Time Square with 2017 New Year Glasses, **Account Number 1231.05** the New Year Eve's Night at Central Park, **Account Number 1231.06** the New Year Eve's Night on a Boat, **Account Number 1231.07** the New Year Eve's Night at the Ice-Skating Rink at the Rockefeller Center, **Account Number 1231.08** the New Year's First Baby Born at Each of the New York City, New York, United States of America Hospitals, **Account Number 1231.09** the New Year Eve's Dances, **Account Number 1231.10** the New Year Eve's Celebrations on Television Every Hour, **Account Number 1231.11** the New Year Eve's Concerts, **Account Number 1231.12** the New Year Eve's Football Games, **Account Number 1231.13** the New Year Eve's Food, **Account Number 1231.14** the New Year's Day Parade, **Account Number 1231.15** the New Year Eve's Fireworks, **Account Number 1231.16** the Midnight Kiss, **Account Number 1231.17** the New Year Eve at an Amusement Park with

Extended Hours, **Account Number 1231.18** the New Year Eve's Night at the Movies, **Account Number 1231.19** the New Year Eve's Night at the Museum, **Account Number 1231.20** the New Year Eve's Night at the Zoo, **Account Number 1231.21** the New Year Eve's Night at Church, **Account Number 1231.22** the New Year Eve's Night in the New York City, New York, United States of America Subway Station, **Account Number 1231.23** the New Year's Resolutions, **Account Number 1231.24** the New Year Eve's Family Night of Games, **Account Number 1231.25** the Clock Strikes Midnight, and **Account Number 1231.26** the Ball Drops at Midnight are sites where the New Year's Resolutions can be made for the New Year.

I, Titus Uno Certified Public Accountant, Forensic Certified Public Accountant, and Chartered Global Management Accountant, and Miss Leah Two, the New York City Mayor Dwight Snowball's Assistant, decided that we would visit the sites where New Year's Resolutions are made in order to be able to approve all of the events that are included in the **Account Number 1231.23** the New Year's Resolutions, a Sub-Account of the **Account Number 1231** the New York Eve's Night in New York City, New York, United States of America. This is a great time for me, Titus Uno Certified Public Accountant, Forensic Certified Public Accountant, and Chartered Global Management Accountant, and Miss Leah Two, the New York City Mayor Dwight Snowball's Assistant, to perform our job and spend time together at the Empire State Building. I, Titus Uno Certified Public Accountant, Forensic Certified Public Accountant, and Chartered Global Management Accountant, and Miss Leah Two, the New York City Mayor Dwight Snowball's Assistant, enjoy spending time together at the sites that the New Year's Resolutions are made. I, Titus Uno Certified Public Accountant, Forensic Certified Public Accountant, and Chartered Global Management Accountant, and Miss Leah Two, the New York City Mayor

Dwight Snowball's Assistant, have to make sure that all of the events at the sites that the New Year's Resolutions are made are up to the best standards so that everyone that attends this part of the **Account Number 1231** the New York Eve's Night in New York City, New York, United States of America will be very happy that they chose this event to bring in the New Year.

"10, 9, 8, 7, 6, 5, 4, 3, 2, 1, Happy New Year." Some families stay up for hours playing board games with each other. Some families play video games until the New Year arrives.

Account Number 1231.24 the New Year Eve's Family Night of Games is the twenty-fourth Sub-Account of the **Account Number 1231** the New York Eve's Night in New York City, New York, United States of America.

The New Year Eve's Family Night of Games includes board games, card games, dominoes, or even video games while watching the partying and the ball dropping in Time Square in New York City, New York, United States of America.

Board games are played by families that usually have the television on tuned into a channel that shows the New York City, New York, United States of America show including the Time Square dropping of the ball.

Card games are played by families that usually have the television on tuned into a channel that shows the New York City, New York, United States of America show including the Time Square dropping of the ball.

Dominoes are played by families that usually have the television on tuned into a channel that shows the New York City, New York, United States of America show including the Time Square dropping of the ball.

Video games are played by families that usually have the television on tuned into a channel that shows the New York City, New York, United States of America show including the Time Square dropping of the ball.

I, Titus Uno Certified Public Accountant, Forensic Certified Public Accountant, and Chartered Global Management Accountant, and Miss Leah Two, the New York City Mayor Dwight Snowball's Assistant, decided that we would visit the television stations in order to be able to approve all of the events that are included in the **Account Number 1231.24** the New Year Eve's Family Night of Games a Sub-Account of the **Account Number 1231** the New York Eve's Night in New York City, New York, United States of America. This is a great time for me, Titus Uno Certified Public Accountant, Forensic Certified Public Accountant, and Chartered Global Management Accountant, and Miss Leah Two, the New York City Mayor Dwight Snowball's Assistant, to perform our job and spend time together at the television stations that families have on while playing the New Year Eve's Family Night of Games. I, Titus Uno Certified Public Accountant, Forensic Certified Public Accountant, and Chartered Global Management Accountant, and Miss Leah Two, the New York City Mayor Dwight Snowball's Assistant, enjoy spending time together at the television stations that families have on while playing the New Year Eve's Family Night of Games. I, Titus Uno Certified Public Accountant, Forensic Certified Public Accountant, and Chartered Global Management Accountant, and Miss Leah Two, the New York City Mayor Dwight Snowball's Assistant, have to make sure that all of the events at the television stations that families have on while playing the New Year Eve's Family Night of Games are up to the best standards so that everyone that attends this part of the **Account**

Number 1231 the New York Eve's Night in New York City, New York, United States of America will be very happy that they chose this event to bring in the New Year.

"10, 9, 8, 7, 6, 5, 4, 3, 2, 1, Happy New Year." Midnight marks the New Year has begun.

Account Number 1231.25 the Clock Strikes Midnight is the twenty-fifth Sub-Account of the **Account Number 1231** the New York Eve's Night in New York City, New York, United States of America.

The following Sub-Accounts: **Account Number 1231.01** the New Year Eve's Night at the Empire State Building, **Account Number 1231.02** the New Year Eve's Night at the One World Observatory, **Account Number 1231.03** the New Year Eve's Night at the Statue of Liberty, **Account Number 1231.04** the New Year Eve's Night at Time Square with 2017 New Year Glasses, **Account Number 1231.05** the New Year Eve's Night at Central Park, **Account Number 1231.06** the New Year Eve's Night on a Boat, **Account Number 1231.07** the New Year Eve's Night at the Ice-Skating Rink at the Rockefeller Center, **Account Number 1231.08** the New Year's First Baby Born at Each of the New York City, New York, United States of America Hospitals, **Account Number 1231.09** the New Year Eve's Dances, **Account Number 1231.10** the New Year Eve's Celebrations on Television Every Hour, **Account Number 1231.11** the New Year Eve's Concerts, **Account Number 1231.12** the New Year Eve's Football Games, **Account Number 1231.13** the New Year Eve's Food, **Account Number 1231.14** the New Year's Day Parade, **Account Number 1231.15** the New Year Eve's Fireworks, **Account Number 1231.16** the Midnight Kiss, **Account Number 1231.17** the New Year Eve at an Amusement Park with Extended Hours, **Account Number 1231.18** the New Year Eve's Night at the Movies, **Account**

Number 1231.19 the New Year Eve's Night at the Museum, **Account Number 1231.20** the New Year Eve's Night at the Zoo, **Account Number 1231.21** the New Year Eve's Night at Church, **Account Number 1231.22** the New Year Eve's Night in the New York City, New York, United States of America Subway Station, **Account Number 1231.23** the New Year's Resolutions, **Account Number 1231.24** the New Year Eve's Family Night of Games, **Account Number 1231.25** the Clock Strikes Midnight, and **Account Number 1231.26** the Ball Drops at Midnight are events that occur around midnight to celebrate the New Year at midnight.

I, Titus Uno Certified Public Accountant, Forensic Certified Public Accountant, and Chartered Global Management Accountant, and Miss Leah Two, the New York City Mayor Dwight Snowball's Assistant, decided that we would visit the most popular sites to be at when the Clock Strikes Midnight in order to be able to approve all of the events that are included in the **Account Number 1231.25** the Clock Strikes Midnight, a Sub-Account of the **Account Number 1231** the New York Eve's Night in New York City, New York, United States of America. This is a great time for me, Titus Uno Certified Public Accountant, Forensic Certified Public Accountant, and Chartered Global Management Accountant, and Miss Leah Two, the New York City Mayor Dwight Snowball's Assistant, to perform our job and spend time together at the most popular sites to be at when the Clock Strikes Midnight. I, Titus Uno Certified Public Accountant, Forensic Certified Public Accountant, and Chartered Global Management Accountant, and Miss Leah Two, the New York City Mayor Dwight Snowball's Assistant, enjoy spending time together at the most popular sites to be at when the Clock Strikes Midnight. I, Titus Uno Certified Public Accountant, Forensic Certified Public Accountant, and Chartered Global Management Accountant, and Miss Leah Two, the New York City Mayor Dwight Snowball's Assistant, have to make sure that all of the events at the most popular sites to be at when the Clock Strikes

Midnight are up to the best standards so that everyone that attends this part of the **Account**

Number 1231 the New York Eve's Night in New York City, New York, United States of America

will be very happy that they chose this event to bring in the New Year.

"10, 9, 8, 7, 6, 5, 4, 3, 2, 1, Happy New Year." The ball drops in New York City, New York, United States of America.

Account Number 1231.26 the Ball Drops at Midnight is the twenty-sixth Sub-Account of the **Account Number 1231** the New York Eve's Night in New York City, New York, United States of America.

The Ball Drops at Midnight as "10, 9, 8, 7, 6, 5, 4, 3, 2, 1, Happy New Year" is chanted by everyone that is in Time Square. All of the couple turn to their date or love and gives them a kiss to start the New Year.

Some of the people in attendance at Time Square wears the cool glasses with the New Year shape. It is so cool to see how many people are in attendance to see the ball drop in Time Square.

"10, 9, 8, 7, 6, 5, 4, 3, 2, 1, Happy New Year."

The following Sub-Accounts: **Account Number 1231.01** the New Year Eve's Night at the Empire State Building, **Account Number 1231.02** the New Year Eve's Night at the One World Observatory, **Account Number 1231.03** the New Year Eve's Night at the Statue of Liberty, **Account Number 1231.04** the New Year Eve's Night at Time Square with 2017 New Year Glasses, **Account Number 1231.05** the New Year Eve's Night at Central Park, **Account Number 1231.06** the New Year Eve's Night on a Boat, **Account Number 1231.07** the New Year Eve's

Night at the Ice-Skating Rink at the Rockefeller Center, **Account Number 1231.08** the New

Year's First Baby Born at Each of the New York City, New York, United States of America

Hospitals, **Account Number 1231.09** the New Year Eve's Dances, **Account Number 1231.10** the

New Year Eve's Celebrations on Television Every Hour, **Account Number 1231.11** the New Year

Eve's Concerts, **Account Number 1231.12** the New Year Eve's Football Games, **Account**

Number 1231.13 the New Year Eve's Food, **Account Number 1231.14** the New Year's Day

Parade, **Account Number 1231.15** the New Year Eve's Fireworks, **Account Number 1231.16** the

Midnight Kiss, **Account Number 1231.17** the New Year Eve at an Amusement Park with

Extended Hours, **Account Number 1231.18** the New Year Eve's Night at the Movies, **Account**

Number 1231.19 the New Year Eve's Night at the Museum, **Account Number 1231.20** the New

Year Eve's Night at the Zoo, **Account Number 1231.21** the New Year Eve's Night at Church,

Account Number 1231.22 the New Year Eve's Night in the New York City, New York, United

States of America Subway Station, **Account Number 1231.23** the New Year's Resolutions,

Account Number 1231.24 the New Year Eve's Family Night of Games, **Account Number**

1231.25 the Clock Strikes Midnight can be attended and the dropping of the ball in Time Square

can still be watched on the cell phones or laptops.

I, Titus Uno Certified Public Accountant, Forensic Certified Public Accountant, and Chartered

Global Management Accountant, and Miss Leah Two, the New York City Mayor Dwight

Snowball's Assistant, decided that we would visit the Time Square in order to be able to

approve all of the events that are included in the **Account Number 1231.26** the Ball Drops at

Midnight, a Sub-Account of the **Account Number 1231** the New York Eve's Night in New York

City, New York, United States of America. This is a great time for me, Titus Uno Certified Public

Accountant, Forensic Certified Public Accountant, and Chartered Global Management Accountant, and Miss Leah Two, the New York City Mayor Dwight Snowball's Assistant, to perform our job and spend time together at the Time Square where the Ball Drops at Midnight. I, Titus Uno Certified Public Accountant, Forensic Certified Public Accountant, and Chartered Global Management Accountant, and Miss Leah Two, the New York City Mayor Dwight Snowball's Assistant, enjoy spending time together at the Time Square where the Ball Drops at Midnight. I, Titus Uno Certified Public Accountant, Forensic Certified Public Accountant, and Chartered Global Management Accountant, and Miss Leah Two, the New York City Mayor Dwight Snowball's Assistant, have to make sure that all of the events at the Time Square where the Ball Drops at Midnight are up to the best standards so that everyone that attends this part of the **Account Number 1231** the New York Eve's Night in New York City, New York, United States of America will be very happy that they chose this event to bring in the New Year.

"10, 9, 8, 7, 6, 5, 4, 3, 2, 1, Happy New Year."

I, Titus Uno Certified Public Accountant, Forensic Certified Public Accountant, and Chartered Global Management Accountant, and Miss Leah Two showed up a Courtroom for the purpose of getting married on New Year's Night. I never imagined that I would be married by 2017 and in New York City, New York, United States of America. The Mayor of New York decided that he would marry Miss Leah Two and myself before the clock struck Midnight. Miss Leah Two had become Mrs. Titus Uno.

This is the most amazing feeling to be part of Mr. And Mrs. Titus Uno. My tax return will now be filled as Married Filing Jointly, not as a single filer.

I, Titus Uno Certified Public Accountant, Forensic Certified Public Accountant, and Chartered Global Management Accountant, proposed to Miss Leah Two while we were at the Empire State Building on the observation deck level. I, Titus Uno Certified Public Accountant, Forensic Certified Public Accountant, and Chartered Global Management Accountant, had the engagement ring placed in some mistletoe and when Miss Leah Two was under this mistletoe, I got down on one knee and asked Miss Leah Two to merry me. Miss Leah Two said, "Yes" without any hesitation. I pointed to the mistletoe with the engagement ring in it. I gave Miss Leah Two, or future Mrs. Titus Uno, a kiss. We got the engagement ring out of the mistletoe. I place the engagement ring on her finger and then gave her another kiss. Wow, I was so excited and happy. I had finally found my future wife.

It sounds great to be able to return home and see everyone and to visit with family and friends. Of course, everyone is getting older. I will be able to relax, since the rest of my Forensic Certified Public Accountant team, Drew Samson – the private investigator, Dena Hope – the computer programmer and hacker, Veronica Jackson – the scheduler, organizer, and item collector, Jack "Sheriff" Starr- CEO or Chief Executive Office, are taking time off, so that they can all spend time with their own families.

It is important that my team spends time with their family since my team has worked hard the entire year. Drew Samson, Dena Hope, Jack Starr, and Veronica Jackson have all decided to spend time with their families in New York City, New York, United States of America. New Years is a time where families gather together and enjoy being around each other to start the New Year together. Families are very important whether you are single, married, separated or divorced, orphaned, or widowed. I, Titus Uno, Certified Public Accountant, Forensic Certified Public Accountant, and Chartered Global Management Accountant, remember when dad, mom, sister, and I would meet at my grandparent's house with all of the other family members to bring in the New Year. That was so much fun. All of the parents would talk, all the children would play. Those afternoons would fly. Families are what life is about to bring in the New Year. That and being nice to others. My grandparents were always so sweet and nice to all their children, grandchildren, and great-grandchildren as the New Year approached. Those were fun days.

First, Drew Samson, the Private Investigator of the Forensic Certified Public Accountant team always enjoys going undercover to gather information for me to help me solve the case. Drew Samson has a beautiful wife, Jill Samson, and 2 children, Simon Samson, a boy, who is ten and

Delilah Samson, a girl, who is 8. Drew Samson works hard to support his family, while having the flexibility to see his children in the activities. It is great that Drew Samson has this job and a family especially at Thanksgiving.

Drew and Jill, and their children: Simon, and Delilah Samson have decided to spend New Year's Day with the Forensic Certified Public Accountant team in New York City, New York, United States of America. So, I say, "Happy New Year in New York City, New York, United States of America, Samson Family."

Second, Dena Hope, the computer programmer and genius of the Forensic Certified Public Accountant team. Dena Hope is single because she spent her time working really hard. That is why Dena Hope is one of the best computer programmers in the world. Dena Hope dedicates all of her free time working on the computer.

Dena Hope is going to spend New York City, New York, United States of America. Her parents, also, arrived at New York City, New York, United States of America. It is awesome to spend as much time with your parents as you can. The older that you get, the more this statement makes sense. Enjoy every minute together that you can. Happy New Year, Dena Hope. You will be glad that you have spent every Thanksgiving with your parents.

Third, Jack "Sheriff" Starr is the Chief Executive Officer of the Forensic Certified Public Accountant team. Jack Starr is a very happily married man. His wife is Jessica Starr. Jack and Jessica are happily married and have been married for Twenty-three wonderful years. They have 5 children: two boys, Jim Starr and Jeff Starr and 3 girls, Janet Starr, Jill Starr, and Joan Starr. Jack and Jessica, Jim, Jeff, Janet, Jill, and Joan Starr all get along with each other and the have fun spending time with each other. They always take an annual family vacation. Over the years they have been to Paris, London, Hawaii, Orlando, Rome, Sydney, Cairo, Rio, Tokyo, Toronto, New York, and Washington, D.C. Jack Starr believes that spending time with his family is his favorite thing to do.

Jack and Jessica, Jim, Jeff, Janet, Jill, and Joan Starr decided to join the Forensic Certified Public Accountant team at New York City, New York, United States of America. There is so much to see at New York City, New York, United States of America.

Fourth, Veronica Jackson, the scheduler, organizer, and item collector for the team. Without her the operations of my team would not be possible. Every team need an organizer and a go getter. Veronica Jackson sets up the meeting and makes sure that we get to that meet on time. Veronica Jackson always helps us appear to be great by keeping up punctual and organized. Veronica Jackson, believe it or not, worked for the President of the United States as one of his secretaries. This may be an important fact in the future. Veronica Jackson is happily married to her husband, Carl Jackson for 24 years. They have a daughter, Rose Jackson that has just graduated from college with a Master's Degree in Accounting. Carl and Veronica Jackson are very proud of Rose Jackson. She already has a job at one of the Big 4 accounting firms in the United States of America. Becoming a successful Certified Public Accountant has always been the goal of Rose Jackson. Veronica Jackson has been training for the Certified Public Accountant Examination for years and especially while she was in college getting an education. I, Titus Uno, have promised Rose Jackson that I will help her in her important journey to become a Certified Public Accountant.

Veronica Jackson and her husband Carl Jackson along with their daughter Rose Jackson have all chosen New York City, New York, United States of America as their New Year's destination.

My entire Forensic Certified Public Accountant team and their families showed up for my wedding. This is what I call perfect timing. I wonder if Santa Claus made this happen. This is awesome to have all these people at my wedding.

My sister, Nine Uno, and her fiancé, Prime Meridian also showed up for my wedding along with my parents Deuce Uno and Trace Uno. Our wedding went so great that my sister, Nine Uno, and her fiancé, Prime Meridian decided to follow our lead. Guess what? We had a double wedding at the City Hall in New York City, New York, United States of America. That is cool that my sister and I will have the same wedding anniversary every year on December 31st. I am so proud of my parents and my sister. It was so important to me that my parents and my sister were present. I bet my sister felt the same way.

Deuce Uno and Trace Uno – Titus and Nine Uno's parents, Star Meridian and Mississippi Meridian – Prime Meridian's parents, and Duet Two and Pair Two –Leah Two's parents, all decided to retake their vows. Wow, talk about romantic. This is the perfect way to end 2016 and bring in 2017. Happy New Year 2017.

After the 2 weddings and the three retaking of the vows, we stayed at the City Hall and all talked and of course took photos, way into the night and into the New Year. However, we later attended some of the following events that Lena, my new wife, and myself attended: **Account Number 1231.01** the New Year Eve's Night at the Empire State Building, **Account Number 1231.02** the New Year Eve's Night at the One World Observatory, **Account Number 1231.03** the New Year Eve's Night at the Statue of Liberty, **Account Number 1231.04** the New Year Eve's Night at Time Square with 2017 New Year Glasses, **Account Number 1231.05** the New Year Eve's Night at Central Park, **Account Number 1231.06** the New Year Eve's Night on a Boat,

Account Number 1231.07 the New Year Eve's Night at the Ice-Skating Rink at the Rockefeller Center, **Account Number 1231.08** the New Year's First Baby Born at Each of the New York City, New York, United States of America Hospitals, **Account Number 1231.09** the New Year Eve's Dances, **Account Number 1231.10** the New Year Eve's Celebrations on Television Every Hour, **Account Number 1231.11** the New Year Eve's Concerts, **Account Number 1231.12** the New Year Eve's Football Games, **Account Number 1231.13** the New Year Eve's Food, **Account Number 1231.14** the New Year's Day Parade, **Account Number 1231.15** the New Year Eve's Fireworks, **Account Number 1231.16** the Midnight Kiss, **Account Number 1231.17** the New Year Eve at an Amusement Park with Extended Hours, **Account Number 1231.18** the New Year Eve's Night at the Movies, **Account Number 1231.19** the New Year Eve's Night at the Museum, **Account Number 1231.20** the New Year Eve's Night at the Zoo, **Account Number 1231.21** the New Year Eve's Night at Church, **Account Number 1231.22** the New Year Eve's Night in the New York City, New York, United States of America Subway Station, **Account Number 1231.23** the New Year's Resolutions, **Account Number 1231.24** the New Year Eve's Family Night of Games, **Account Number 1231.25** the Clock Strikes Midnight, and **Account Number 1231.26** the Ball Drops at Midnight. The New York City Mayor Dwight Snowball did a great performance with all of the ceremonies. Mayor Dwight that was the most fun he has ever had marrying everyone tonight. New York Mayor Dwight Snowball's wife, Coconut Snowball was in attendance. Their children were in attendance also, their son Dwight C. Snowball and their daughter, Coco Snowball.

Mayor Dwight Snowball and his family all left the New York City Hall to go to Time Square so that he could it the button to start the New Year's Ball drop in Time Square. "Ten, nine, eight, seven, six, five, four, three, two, one, Happy New Year."

Wow, what a wonderful year. "10, 9, 8, 7, 6, 5, 4, 3, 2, 1, Happy New Year." The newly married Titus Uno, Certified Public Accountant, Forensic Certified Public Accountant, and Chartered Global Management Accountant, is really happy about this New Year's Night. Marriage means that Titus Uno, Certified Public Accountant, Forensic Certified Public Accountant, and Chartered Global Management Accountant has someone else to take care of and someone else to take care of him. That is so awesome being a Newlywed. Both sides of the family will want little babies added to the Uno family.

Account Number 1231.01 the New Year Eve's Night at the Empire State Building is the first Sub-Account of the **Account Number 1231** the New York Eve's Night in New York City, New York, United States of America. The **Account Number 1231.01** the New Year Eve's Night at the Empire State Building was a complete successes and was accurately accounted for by the **Account Number 1231** the New York Eve's Night in New York City, New York, United States of America Committee and by Leah Uno, my new wife.

Account Number 1231.02 the New Year Eve's Night at the One World Observatory, is the second Sub-Account of the **Account Number 1231** the New York Eve's Night in New York City, New York, United States of America. The **Account Number 1231.02** the New Year Eve's Night at the One World Observatory was a complete successes and was accurately accounted for by the **Account Number 1231** the New York Eve's Night in New York City, New York, United States of America Committee and by Leah Uno, my new wife.

Account Number 1231.03 the New Year Eve's Night at the Statue of Liberty is the third Sub-Account of the **Account Number 1231** the New York Eve's Night in New York City, New York, United States of America. The **Account Number 1231.03** the New Year Eve's Night at the Statue of Liberty was a complete successes and was accurately accounted for by the **Account Number 1231** the New York Eve's Night in New York City, New York, United States of America Committee and by Leah Uno, my new wife.

Account Number 1231.04 the New Year Eve's Night at Time Square with 2017 New Year Glasses is the fourth Sub-Account of the **Account Number 1231** the New York Eve's Night in New York City, New York, United States of America. The **Account Number 1231.04** the New Year Eve's Night at Time Square with 2017 New Year Glasses was a complete successes and was accurately accounted for by the **Account Number 1231** the New York Eve's Night in New York City, New York, United States of America Committee and by Leah Uno, my new wife.

Account Number 1231.05 the New Year Eve's Night at Central Park is the fifth Sub-Account of the **Account Number 1231** the New York Eve's Night in New York City, New York, United States of America. The **Account Number 1231.05** the New Year Eve's Night at Central Park was a complete successes and was accurately accounted for by the **Account Number 1231** the New York Eve's Night in New York City, New York, United States of America Committee and by Leah Uno, my new wife.

Account Number 1231.06 the New Year Eve's Night on a Boat Airplane, Helicopter, or even a Blimp is the sixth Sub-Account of the **Account Number 1231** the New York Eve's Night in New York City, New York, United States of America. The **Account Number 1231.06** the New Year Eve's Night on a Boat Airplane, Helicopter, or even a Blimp was a complete successes and was accurately accounted for by the **Account Number 1231** the New York Eve's Night in New York City, New York, United States of America Committee and by Leah Uno, my new wife.

Account Number 1231.07 the New Year Eve's Night at the Ice-Skating Rink at the Rockefeller Center is the seventh Sub-Account of the **Account Number 1231** the New York Eve's Night in New York City, New York, United States of America. The **Account Number 1231.07** the New Year Eve's Night at the Ice-Skating Rink at the Rockefeller Center was a complete successes and was accurately accounted for by the **Account Number 1231** the New York Eve's Night in New York City, New York, United States of America Committee and by Leah Uno, my new wife.

Account Number 1231.08 the New Year's First Baby Born at Each of the New York City, New York, United States of America Hospitals is the eighth Sub-Account of the **Account Number 1231** the New York Eve's Night in New York City, New York, United States of America. The **Account Number 1231.08** the New Year's First Baby Born at Each of the New York City, New York, United States of America Hospitals was a complete successes and was accurately accounted for by the **Account Number 1231** the New York Eve's Night in New York City, New York, United States of America Committee and by Leah Uno, my new wife.

Account Number 1231.09 the New Year Eve's Dances is the ninth Sub-Account of the **Account Number 1231** the New York Eve's Night in New York City, New York, United States of

America. The **Account Number 1231.09** the New Year Eve's Dances was a complete successes and was accurately accounted for by the **Account Number 1231** the New York Eve's Night in New York City, New York, United States of America Committee and by Leah Uno, my new wife.

Account Number 1231.10 the New Year Eve's Celebrations on Television Every Hour is the tenth Sub-Account of the **Account Number 1231** the New York Eve's Night in New York City, New York, United States of America. The **Account Number 1231.10** the New Year Eve's Celebrations on Television Every Hour was a complete successes and was accurately accounted for by the **Account Number 1231** the New York Eve's Night in New York City, New York, United States of America Committee and by Leah Uno, my new wife.

Account Number 1231.11 the New Year Eve's Concerts is the eleventh Sub-Account of the **Account Number 1231** the New York Eve's Night in New York City, New York, United States of America. The **Account Number 1231.11** the New Year Eve's Concerts was a complete successes and was accurately accounted for by the **Account Number 1231** the New York Eve's Night in New York City, New York, United States of America Committee and by Leah Uno, my new wife.

Account Number 1231.12 the New Year Eve's Football Games is the twelfth Sub-Account of the **Account Number 1231** the New York Eve's Night in New York City, New York, United States of America. The **Account Number 1231.12** the New Year Eve's Football Games was a complete successes and was accurately accounted for by the **Account Number 1231** the New York Eve's Night in New York City, New York, United States of America Committee and by Leah Uno, my new wife.

Account Number 1231.13 the New Year Eve's Food is the thirteenth Sub-Account of the **Account Number 1231** the New York Eve's Night in New York City, New York, United States of America. The **Account Number 1231.13** the New Year Eve's Food was a complete successes and was accurately accounted for by the **Account Number 1231** the New York Eve's Night in New York City, New York, United States of America Committee and by Leah Uno, my new wife.

Account Number 1231.14 the New Year's Day Parade is the fourteenth Sub-Account of the **Account Number 1231** the New York Eve's Night in New York City, New York, United States of America. The **Account Number 1231.14** the New Year's Day Parade was a complete successes and was accurately accounted for by the **Account Number 1231** the New York Eve's Night in New York City, New York, United States of America Committee and by Leah Uno, my new wife.

Account Number 1231.15 the New Year Eve's Fireworks is the fifteenth Sub-Account of the **Account Number 1231** the New York Eve's Night in New York City, New York, United States of America. The **Account Number 1231.15** the New Year Eve's Fireworks was a complete successes and was accurately accounted for by the **Account Number 1231** the New York Eve's Night in New York City, New York, United States of America Committee and by Leah Uno, my new wife.

Account Number 1231.16 the Midnight Kiss is the sixteenth Sub-Account of the **Account Number 1231** the New York Eve's Night in New York City, New York, United States of America. The **Account Number 1231.16** the Midnight Kiss was a complete successes and was accurately accounted for by the **Account Number 1231** the New York Eve's Night in New York City, New York, United States of America Committee and by Leah Uno, my new wife.

Account Number 1231.17 the New Year Eve at an Amusement Park with Extended Hours is the seventeenth Sub-Account of the **Account Number 1231** the New York Eve's Night in New York City, New York, United States of America. The **Account Number 1231.17** the New Year Eve at an Amusement Park with Extended Hours was a complete successes and was accurately accounted for by the **Account Number 1231** the New York Eve's Night in New York City, New York, United States of America Committee and by Leah Uno, my new wife.

Account Number 1231.18 the New Year Eve's Night at the Movies is the eighteenth Sub-Account of the **Account Number 1231** the New York Eve's Night in New York City, New York, United States of America. The **Account Number 1231.18** the New Year Eve's Night at the Movies was a complete successes and was accurately accounted for by the **Account Number 1231** the New York Eve's Night in New York City, New York, United States of America Committee and by Leah Uno, my new wife.

Account Number 1231.19 the New Year Eve's Night at the Museum is the nineteenth Sub-Account of the **Account Number 1231** the New York Eve's Night in New York City, New York, United States of America. The **Account Number 1231.19** the New Year Eve's Night at the Museum was a complete successes and was accurately accounted for by the **Account Number 1231** the New York Eve's Night in New York City, New York, United States of America Committee and by Leah Uno, my new wife.

Account Number 1231.20 the New Year Eve's Night at the Zoo is the twentieth Sub-Account of the **Account Number 1231** the New York Eve's Night in New York City, New York, United States of America. The **Account Number 1231.20** the New Year Eve's Night at the Zoo was a complete successes and was accurately accounted for by the **Account Number 1231** the New York Eve's Night in New York City, New York, United States of America Committee and by Leah Uno, my new wife.

Account Number 1231.21 the New Year Eve's Night at Church is the twenty-first Sub-Account of the **Account Number 1231** the New York Eve's Night in New York City, New York, United States of America. The **Account Number 1231.21** the New Year Eve's Night at Church was a complete successes and was accurately accounted for by the **Account Number 1231** the New York Eve's Night in New York City, New York, United States of America Committee and by Leah Uno, my new wife.

Account Number 1231.22 the New Year Eve's Night in the New York City, New York, United States of America Subway Station is the twenty-second Sub-Account of the **Account Number 1231** the New York Eve's Night in New York City, New York, United States of America. The **Account Number 1231.22** the New Year Eve's Night in the New York City, New York, United States of America Subway Station was a complete successes and was accurately accounted for by the **Account Number 1231** the New York Eve's Night in New York City, New York, United States of America Committee and by Leah Uno, my new wife.

Account Number 1231.23 the New Year's Resolutions is the twenty-third Sub-Account of the **Account Number 1231** the New York Eve's Night in New York City, New York, United States of America. The **Account Number 1231.23** the New Year's Resolutions was a complete successes and was accurately accounted for by the **Account Number 1231** the New York Eve's Night in New York City, New York, United States of America Committee and by Leah Uno, my new wife.

Account Number 1231.24 the New Year Eve's Family Night of Games is the twenty-fourth Sub-Account of the **Account Number 1231** the New York Eve's Night in New York City, New York, United States of America. The **Account Number 1231.24** the New Year Eve's Family Night of Games was a complete successes and was accurately accounted for by the **Account Number 1231** the New York Eve's Night in New York City, New York, United States of America Committee and by Leah Uno, my new wife.

Account Number 1231.25 the Clock Strikes Midnight is the twenty-fifth Sub-Account of the **Account Number 1231** the New York Eve's Night in New York City, New York, United States of America. The **Account Number 1231.25** the Clock Strikes Midnight was a complete successes and was accurately accounted for by the **Account Number 1231** the New York Eve's Night in New York City, New York, United States of America Committee and by Leah Uno, my new wife.

Account Number 1231.26 the Ball Drops at Midnight is the twenty-sixth Sub-Account of the **Account Number 1231** the New York Eve's Night in New York City, New York, United States of America. The **Account Number 1231.26** the Ball Drops at Midnight was a complete successes and was accurately accounted for by the **Account Number 1231** the New York Eve's Night in New York City, New York, United States of America Committee and by Leah Uno, my new wife.

Happy New Year, readers.

www.ingramcontent.com/pod-product-compliance
Lightning Source LLC
Chambersburg PA
CBHW081313170526
45166CB00011B/3506